UNDERSTANDING INVESTMENT   Ephraim Unuigbe

UNDERSTANDING INVESTMENT

FOR BEGINNERS

EPHRAIM UNUIGBE (ACA)

UNDERSTANDING INVESTMENT

For Beginners

EPHRAIM UNUIGBE (ACA)

Copyright October 2022 © **Ephraim Unuigbe**

All rights reserved.

No part of this book may be reproduced, distributed, stored, or transmitted in any form or by any means, including electronic, photocopy, recording, producing, or resale without the prior written permission of the author and publisher, except in the case of brief quotations embodied in reviews and articles as well as specific other non-commercial uses permitted by copyright law.

Contact the author via info@ephraim-unuigbe.online; ephraim.unuigbe@gmail.com.

DEDICATION

To God. Thank you.

TABLE OF CONTENTS

Dedication

Preface

Disclaimer

Chapter 1: What Investment is and is not..........................11

Chapter 2: To Hold Cash or Not. 29

Chapter 3: Different Investment Types 39

Chapter 4: Understanding Investment Patterns....................62

Chapter 5: Managing Investment Risk..............................71

Chapter 6: Funds Categorization.......................................82

Chapter 7: Common Pitfalls In Investing............................97

About The Book...109

About The Author..111

Acknowledgments..112

Other Books by the Author to date.....................................113

Services We Offer..114

PREFACE

Investing is a vehicle through which you can overcome the limitations of time. It is not the time itself that is limited but the amount of time people have at their disposal. We must invest for this reason.

No matter how much a person earns, they will never be able to meet their needs if paid by the hour. In economics, it is said that human needs are limitless, but the means of meeting those needs are not. Consequently, some people work additional shifts or hours to meet those needs. However, due to limited available time, it's advisable that they devise a method to ensure that their money is secure and productive while they are not actively engaged in employment.

As a career professional, therefore, if you do not invest your money, you are likely to work until you are too old. Please don't wait until it is too late. Get started now and take advantage of compound interest. As far as I know, the stock market is one of the best places to invest your money, as it gives an average return of 8% pa if you invest in ETFs instead of individual stocks over a long time.

People with no finance background may find this too complex, but in this book, I simplify complicated terms to make them accessible.

DISCLAIMER

The content of this book does not constitute legal, tax, accounting, financial, or investment advice. For information relating to your specific circumstances, you are encouraged to consult with a competent legal, tax, accounting, financial, or investment professional. In addition to making no warranties as to the accuracy or completeness of this information, I do not endorse any third-party companies, products, or services described here and are not liable for any harm resulting from your use of this information.

Keep in mind that investing involves risk. The value of your investment may fluctuate over time, and you may lose or gain money. Therefore, diversification cannot guarantee against loss or guarantee profit.

CHAPTER ONE

WHAT INVESTMENT IS AND IS NOT

It is a fact that all individuals have access to 24 hours each day, regardless of age, wealth, size, career professional, or businessperson. However, our activities within those 24 hours distinguish us from each other. At that same time, many people have gained advantages that have enabled them to transform their ordinary lives into extraordinary ones.

Those who earn their salary per hour will have difficulty making much more than they desire since their hourly wage is fixed. Even though this amount increases over time, it still is limited since a person's working hours can be defined. Therefore, no matter how many overtime hours are worked, there is still a limit.

With investment, individuals can continue earning income while they are sleeping. Investment eliminates the time constraints described above. The salary earner continues earning income unconsciously regardless of whether they want to do so. They continue earning income even while they are still performing their regular work.

As a result of investing, that time challenge is overcome, and the limitation of earning above what a person can generally make is removed. This is mainly because they are not directly involved. In essence, money is allowed to multiply itself without obvious time restraints, and the individual is able to earn an unlimited amount of money. This becomes an almost limitless source of income for them. The benefits are numerous, and because of the advantages that investment offers, some people will not need to work much over time. As a result, people can choose whether to work from 9 am to 5 pm for 8 hours every day, 10 am to 2 pm for 4 hours every day, or 9 am to 12 for 3 hours every day. In some cases, individuals may elect to altogether resign from their jobs to more time on other interests that are not related to their professional careers when the return on their investment exceeds the income they earn from their job.

If a person earns a fixed salary of £50k per annum and consistently saves £10k from that income, they will have accumulated £50k after five years as savings. However, if that £10k were invested yearly in an investment that yields an annual return of 10%, then at the end of year one, they would have an additional £1k. At the end of year two, they would have an additional £2k from the £10k investment in year one and another £1k from the £10k investment in year two, making the total investment at the end of year two $3k.

During the third year, they would have accumulated £3k from the £10k investment in year one, £2k total from the £10k investment in year two, and £1k from the £10k investment in year three, resulting in total returns on investment of £6k (i.e., 3k + 2k + 1k). If this continues until the end of the fifth year, the individual will have a total of £65k, which is the total of £50k savings and the 15k return on investment, totaling £65k.

In this example, we have used the numbers solely for illustration purposes and to provide you with a general understanding of how the investment works and also how to utilize its potential. The annual returns in a real-life situation will be plowed back to provide even higher returns. Also, depending on where you live, the rate of return may be less than or greater than 10%.

There are several advantages to investing and some misconceptions about investing that we will discuss.

Advantages of investment

Investing has many advantages, but we will discuss five of them in this chapter, but it is important to note that there are many more.

Your Money Works for You When You Invest

Investing is a way to make your money work harder for you. As you may have seen from our example above, a person earning £50k and saving £10k per year acquires an additional £15k due to compound interest. By investing, this individual has increased the value of their money. Conversely, the individual who did not invest will only have £50k by year five.

Investing Is a Method of Accumulating Long-Term Wealth

Investing serves as a long-term savings solution. As you age, you will not be able to maintain the same energy level you have for the rest of your life. At some point, your physical and mental strength will diminish, making it impossible for you to continue performing your current duties. Consequently, taking advantage of the opportunity offered by investment provides individuals with the long-term savings they require.

Investing Allows You to Retire Early and Comfortably

People typically do their jobs for necessity, not necessarily because they love their jobs. Investments provide the option of retiring early. Given the opportunity, many would prefer to travel the world or work less so that they may be able to save some time to do precisely what they desire. Investing allows for this opportunity. By putting aside more money today in high-yielding investments, one can accumulate enough to retire in a reasonable amount of time.

Anyone Can Invest, and it is Flexible.

Investing has become more accessible in recent years thanks to many online platforms that allow you to invest. In the past, investment was reserved for highly technical and specialized individuals who then took a commission in return for helping you invest. Nowadays, one can make very profitable investments from the comfort of their home through their mobile phone or computer. This is a flexibility advantage that one can take advantage of to gain the benefit of investing.

A discussion of the different investment platforms and options individuals can engage in to gain all or some of the advantages we discussed in this chapter will follow further in this book.

Investing Allows You to Achieve Your Goals

You can choose what you want to do when you have a profitable investment. Humanity's number one need is the need for control. People want to have the opportunity to choose the direction of their lives. They want to make decisions on their terms without needing authorization from anyone. People want to have control over their lives.

Except for those who have inherited a large sum, there are few opportunities in this world to acquire financial freedom and achieve other forms of freedom.

Some Misbeliefs about Investment

There are some common false beliefs about investment that many people hold. In the following paragraphs, we shall highlight them and suggest ways to overcome these beliefs.

A Misbelief That Investment is Too Risky

There is a common misconception among some people that investing is always risky. It is far from the case that investment is always tricky. Investments can be risky, but many investments are low risk. It is essential to understand that there are three categories of risks - low, medium, and high risk. The same is valid with risks associated with investing, and what determines a person's level of return is the level of risk they are prepared to undertake.

As a result, even if you are a risk-averse individual, you can still invest in low-risk investments and earn a reasonable return. The same applies to a risk-tolerant individual. Risk tolerance is often considered to be the opposite of risk aversion. The individual can tolerate risk as implied.

If one is meticulous enough to choose their investment consciously, it will save them a lot of money and reduce their losses in the long run. Being a risk-averse individual is not a disadvantage. It would be best if you were consistent with your approach regardless of whether you are risk tolerant or risk averse by investing in situations aligned with your personality, irrespective of whether you are risk-tolerant or risk-averse.

A Misbelief that Investment is for Experts

Investing used to be considered complicated, but since the advent of technology, the free flow of information, apps, and the internet, it is now simple as it was in the past. An app on your smartphone can enable you to make a good profit on any investment throughout the world.

For reliable investment Apps that you can use, you can conduct an internet search depending on your country of residence.

There are also other types of investments covered in this book as we have not limited ourselves to Internet-based investments, but we have focused more on investing in stocks and shares. The various types of investments and how to approach them will be discussed in later chapters.

A Misbelief That Investment is For Others

Some people believe that investment is for others and not for themselves. The belief may be based on their background, the experience of others, or even on their own. They have now concluded that they are not cut out for investment. However, this belief is incorrect.

You do not need a negative experience to conclude that investing is not for you, and even if you had tried it before and got your fingers burnt, that does not suffice to conclude that it is not for everyone. You can direct your investment to the best one by understanding your risk appetite (low, medium, or high risk), as I mentioned previously.

As a child, you attempted to walk again and again until you mastered the technique, and today you can run. This is the same for investing. You may have to try again and again to achieve success.

A Misbelief That Investment is Gambling

investment is often misunderstood as a form of gambling. I found this to be humorous, but it is a false belief. According to Britannica.com, Gambling is betting or staking something of value, with awareness of the risk and the hope of gain, on the outcome of a game, contest, or uncertain event. The outcome may be determined by chance, accident, or unexpected due to the bettor's miscalculation.

A critical examination of this definition will demonstrate that gambling relies on the result of chance or accident. Investment, on the other hand, is based on well-informed calculations. Therefore, it is highly recommended that an individual study an opportunity first before investing in it. Otherwise, one may be gambling. It is also important to note that gambling is a short-lived activity instead of investing, which can last a lifetime. In this book, we will discuss the rules of investment.

A Misbelief That Investment is For the Rich

Some people believe that investment belongs to the wealthy. As you may already know, the rich invest in stocks, start businesses, and invest in real estate. These are the most common avenues for investing for the wealthy. Although an ordinary person may also be an investor, investing is not an exclusive right of the rich.

Investments have made many ordinary people wealthy, and it has become common practice for young people worldwide to invest in businesses outside their national borders.

It is important to note that an individual can and is encouraged to begin investing from where they are. However, it is okay to wait until one has everything in place before investing, as investing works with time. It is, therefore, advisable to begin investing immediately to take advantage of the advantage that starting early provides.

There are other misperceptions, for example, that you need to monitor your investments daily, lock your money away, or believe it is a quick way to make money or that you have to know when it is an excellent time to buy or that you need much time to research.

Even though some of these statements may appear to have some element of truth, none are absolute truths. It would be best if you understood what you wish to invest in and decided to invest. However, as you will find out later in this book, you may not even need to understand some investments in order to succeed.

Although I agree that there are many unprofitable investments out there, you can invest in many profitable ones without too much difficulty.

CHAPTER ONE SUMMARY

Key points to keep in mind

- Investing is not too complicated
- Investing is high risk, and you can lose your money.
- Investing is a way to make your money work for you
- Can easily be done through online platforms and investment apps
- Investing is a long-term savings solution.

CHAPTER TWO
TO HOLD CASH OR NOT

Our discussion in chapter one discussed that investments are vehicles that allow individuals to make their money work harder for them. This chapter will examine some elements and investments and how they differ from cash.

The question may occur to you as to why such information is necessary. Still, it is vital to understand these elements in order to choose a proper investment and savings strategy. The information will serve as a foundation for your investment decision.

Understanding Cash

Historically, cash has been used to exchange goods and services and settle debts. Generally, there will be other reasons for holding money in real life, but in economics, there are three primary reasons, namely transactional reasons, speculative reasons, and precautionary reasons. Other reasons will fall into these three broad categories.

The transaction motive entails the holding of cash for daily needs. Essentially, it is held to exchange cash for things we need and does not possess. The speculative motive for holding cash is so that one can take advantage of any means by which they can multiply their money or increase its value. Lastly, precautionary motives refer to holding money in anticipation of unexpected events. A specific sum of money can go a long way to help you meet these unexpected expenses, and experts recommend setting aside a certain amount periodically.

As noted in chapter one, the need for money will always exceed the amount earned. Otherwise, the highly wealthy individual will not continue seeking. We do not simply need money for the things it can provide us but also for the feeling it gives. If you give this some thought, you will agree that sometimes the fact that you have money gives you some satisfaction, not because you desire to spend it, but simply because it exists.

The feeling of being able to hold excess money in liquid form can be counterproductive. Therefore, it is necessary to have a sense of how much money is required at any given moment. I typically recommend that people have a budget in order to monitor their income and expenditures. However, developing a budget can be a flexible and accurate exercise. The budget should also serve as a guide to determine when and where you will have excess cash.

Having said that, how should excess cash be utilized? This is one of the arguments for investing. We will consider this discussion much later in our discussion of the elements of investment. For now, let's see what happens to idle cash.

Generally, when we describe cash left idle, we assume it is in your bank account, not your home safe. Even though the interest on money left idle can still be earned by an account, it usually yields a lower interest rate. If an individual leaves all their income in an account, they incur a loss.

The interest income generated by the funds in your accounts is eroded by inflation and the risk of exchange rate losses in countries where the exchange rate is highly volatile.

Accordingly, interest income from a regular savings account in the UK currently amounts to less than 1%, while inflation is over 10%. Therefore, as a result of your £2,000 paying you £20 (1% of £2,000), per year, your £2,000's value (the value that money can buy) will decrease to $1,800 (10% of £2,000) at the end of the year. There are some countries where it is even worse. Essentially, you have £1,820 left, which represents interest income less inflationary effects.

Based on the analysis above, there is still some hope that the cash linked to your bank account will increase if the interest income rate increases to 5%, unlike the cash kept in a safe.

Element of Investing

With the understanding of cash and the limitation of holding physical cash, you will agree that it is more profitable to have your excess cash in an investment vehicle.

It is essential to recognize that investing involves various factors, including being linked to the stock market (explained in chapter four), the lack of a guaranteed outcome, and the risk of your funds. Even so, capital market investments have historically outperformed interest rates and inflation over time and are more advantageous than conventional forms of storing cash.

Several types of funds exist, but we will focus on three of them.

- **Money Market Funds**

    These are investments in government bonds, treasury bills, commercial paper, and certificates of deposit. They are primarily short-term investment strategies. Investing in mutual funds allows you to pool your money together with other investors in order to buy a variety of stocks, bonds, or other investments that might not be possible to purchase on your own.

Mutual funds that invest in government bonds provide fixed-income returns, whereas those that invest in equity funds provide variable returns. As a result, the returns of fixed-income mutual funds are usually lower than those of equity mutual funds, although they provide a guaranteed fixed return. In addition, since equity mutual funds have the possibility of capital loss, they are naturally more risky than fixed-income mutual funds.

- **Balanced Funds**

    These are funds invested in a mix of equities and fixed-income securities. Fund managers manage them, and they can combine an appropriate blend of the two for investors that want to combine both high and low-risk funds. As you may have guessed, the returns on this mutual fund are usually higher than those fixed-income funds but lower than the equity fund.

- **Index Funds**

Another essential type of mutual fund is Index Fund. Index Funds are also called ETFs in this book, but they are very different in essence. In general, they consist of a collection of shares or stocks that have specific characteristics. In the next chapter, we will discuss these funds in detail and why they make an excellent investment for beginners.

CHAPTER TWO SUMMARY

Key points to keep in mind

- Budgeting can also help you know how much money you can keep as cash
- Cash in a safe, may not be the best idea
- Inflation can erode the cash linked to your account.
- There are three broad reasons for holding cash transactions, precautionary and speculative reasons.
- Investing is high risk, and you can lose your money.

CHAPTER THREE
DIFFERENT INVESTMENT TYPES

You may have understood that investment is a vast field after reading the last two chapters, where we have explored what investment is and its characteristics. Our goal in this chapter is to examine the various types of investments and how to maximize the returns that can be obtained from these investments. Stocks, shares, property, gold, cryptocurrencies, and non-fungible tokens (NFTs) are some of these investments we will be discussing.

All these investments can be classified as passive investments; you may continue working and earn returns from them. However, they can be converted to active investments, which is a situation in which you are committing your entire time to a particular investment while resigning from your regular position.

People are most familiar with the type of investment known as shares, also known as stocks. While stocks are the more general, generic term, it is often used to describe a slice of ownership of one or more companies, and shares have a more specific meaning: the right of a particular company. Generally, both are used interchangeably to mean the same thing – owning a piece of a company.

Owning a piece of a company for very little money is a brilliant idea. Kudos must go to whoever developed this concept. In essence, it allows you to avoid registering and thinking about what to produce and sell, marketing, employees, and all other associated costs associated with operating a business by simply purchasing some shares of the company and beginning to earn income immediately.

You will realize this importance if you reflect on it long enough. The alternative to your regular job would have been to start your own company, and we know how difficult it would have been to combine both. We spoke about the limited time we have, and investing in shares enables you to save all that time so that you can focus on your daily activities and your 9 to 5. As a result, you can invest in as many companies as you wish, based on your preferences, with a very small amount of funds.

How To Invest in Shares

As this is a beginner's guide to investment, I assume you are not an expert and have no knowledge about how the market works. Additionally, I assume you do not know anything about financing, financial statements, or other related terms. As such, you will most likely not know which companies to invest in if this is the case.

Buying Individual Shares

In a nutshell, if you are a beginner, you should not invest in single shares. What I mean is that you should not buy individual shares of Tesla, Apple, Microsoft, or Meta (Facebook). Instead, you should purchase ETFs or index funds.

The term ETF stands for Exchange Traded Funds, and it is like a group of stocks collected into one bucket. It is similar to a music playlist, where you store all your favorite songs and listen to them only when you feel their quality is the highest. In the same way, instead of purchasing single shares in a particular industry, for example, Tesla or Apple, based on my earlier example (see previous page), you can create a "playlist" of shares from other industries – such as healthcare, real estate, consumer staples, consumer discretionary, utilities, energy, industrials, consumer services, financials, and technology – that you can use when investing.

The share index is a measure of the current state of the stock market by combining the share prices of several companies. For simplicity, we will refer to both share indices and ETFs as ETFs since they both serve the same objective.

Investing in exchange-traded funds (ETFs) has become increasingly popular among new investors looking to build a diversified but low-cost portfolio. However, different types of ETFs offer varying levels of risk, so it is essential to understand how they work before investing.

Among the most popular ETFs is the S&P 500. This ETF contains the top 500 companies in the United States from various industries. Having a piece of this

ETF means that at any given moment, you are investing in the top 500 companies simultaneously. There are numerous benefits to this approach. Among the other US ETFs are the S&P 100, Dow Jones Industrial Average, and Nasdaq Composite.

The FTSE 100 is another example. This index comprises the top 100 companies listed on the London Stock Exchange. "FTSE" is short for "Financial Times Stock Exchange," which is derived from the names of two companies that launched the index: "Financial Times" and "London Stock Exchange." Other UK indices include the FTSE 250, FTSE 350, FTSE SmallCap, and FTSE All-Share. The number of stocks in the index is represented by the '100' in FTSE 100.

Some Advantages of Indices/ETFs

- One can spread their risks across various sectors in order to ensure a well-diversified portfolio.

- Investing in these mutual funds is significantly more affordable than investing in individual companies or other actively managed funds.

- In light of the fact that the shares are listed on an active stock market, one is able to purchase and sell them at any time, allowing an investor to build and rebalance their portfolio relatively quickly and easily.

- The average return on indices/ETFs is generally believed to be 9% per annum over the long run.

- A number of free investment apps are available for people with limited or no knowledge of investing. Some popular ones in the UK are Trading212, Etoro, Wealthify, Capital.com, Freetrade, and so on. Searching the internet for "investment apps" in your country will provide you with a number of excellent and reliable options. However, before making any financial commitments, ensure they are authorized and trustworthy.

You should, however, carefully consider any app prior to making a choice. Remember that your investments are still at risk. As with other investments, you could lose more than you initially invested.

Property Investment

Investment in real estate is the earliest and most lucrative form of investment over time. Yet, despite the apparent fact that this realization is not widely known, many people still need to learn about its significance. Land and buildings, the primary property elements, are found wherever you are in the world, regardless of where you live.

The acquisition of land and property has been a dilemma for humans since the beginning of time. If you take a moment to contemplate this, you will understand why. The reason is reasonable, except in a few cases where there are apparent exceptions; the value of property always appreciates regardless of its location.

As opposed to other investment strategies that can provide a quick profit, real estate is a long-term strategy. As a result, property prices rise steadily for years before they are sold for a substantial profit.

It is important to note that investing in property can provide a range of benefits, including a positive cash flow to help maintain financial stability, a chance to accumulate capital gains, and the possibility of enjoying tax benefits.

It appears prudent to invest in the buy-to-let market, for example, as the population continues to increase and living trends indicate an increasing demand for rental housing. However, even though renting is associated with many advantages, there are also several risks that should be considered.

Some Characteristics of Property

It is reasonable to assume that some of the characteristics of real estate can be deduced from the above paragraphs. To be specific, we have outlined them below.

- **Long-Term**

    Investing in property is long-term, and if you wish to make a significant return on investment, you should do so over the long term. For example, a house worth £1 million in the 90s will be worth more than £10 million in 2022.

- **Significant returns**

   As a general rule, the returns on investment are substantial. As a result, property values can appreciate significantly in a short period of time. As a result, all else being equal, the property's value will also increase.

- **High Risks**

   Investments have tremendous potential for returns and benefits, but some risks are also involved. Therefore, it is essential to remember that the higher returns on an investment, the higher the associated risks.

- **A Source of Passive income**

    As a passive income source, it generates a steady stream of income. This allows you to maintain your day-to-day routine and earn additional income from property simultaneously.

- **Scarcity**

    Due to this reason, the value of property is constantly increasing. In many countries, demand for property is always higher than supply. This means that the number of property seekers is always more significant than the number of available properties.

How To Invest in Property

- **Research**

    Do your research to familiarize yourself with the necessary information about the property before making any decision. Do a background check on the current owner. Ask others around the neighborhood questions if that's possible.

- **Know the risks**

    Each property has a different risk, even in the exact location. Find out what makes one property distinct from the other.

- **Plan Your Strategy**

    Even when you know about a property and the risk, not all property is worth investing in. It would be best if you had a plan for how you want to invest. You should invest in different locations or a specific type of property or even just apartments, for example. Will you be buying to let or to sell? Or will you be interested in commercial properties instead? These are profitable property investment strategies that you need to decide on, and you can gradually combine any of the strategy as you become more experiences.

- **Involve Relevant Experts**

    One expert that you must pay attention to is a solicitor. Ensure you only transact property deals after speaking to a solicitor, no matter how insignificant you think the investment is worth. This will save you a lot of unnecessary stress later.

- **Other Factors**

    Take into account other factors that may contribute to the appreciation of the property, such as a low crime rate, high-grade schools, and access to other social amenities. In addition, consider the history, convenience, and reputation of the environment.

Investment is Gold

Aside from property, gold is the second oldest form of investment. However, I do not consider gold an investment per se but rather a type of store of value. As a result, I will not encourage any new entrant into the investment world to make any investment in gold except if they wish to avoid depreciation or loss of value to their capital. Furthermore, it is only more appropriate to invest in gold during times of economic uncertainty and instability than in other assets.

We explained earlier that cash in its liquid state (physical cash in hand) loses value if it is not spent immediately; therefore, if you wish to maintain the value of your money in the future, you must invest it in an investment that generates a return. In economics, inflation is the term used to describe this phenomenon.

As one of the most popular precious metals, gold is a popular investment option. However, it is essential to note that gold's price has maintained its value over the long term despite being volatile in the short term. Historically, it has provided a hedge against inflation, as well as the erosion of major currencies, so it may be worthwhile to consider.

Crypto-currency and non-fungible token (NFT)
I decided to explain both crypto-currencies and non-fungible tokens (NFT) because I consider them similar – unclear. However, these two investments are unclear to new beginner investors, so I recommend avoiding them and focusing on the other three investments mentioned earlier. In both cases, you will either need more time to research, or you will be making blind investments. This is primarily due to the fact that your desire to invest will be based on the experiences of others rather than on a proper understanding of what they are and how they work.

Cryptocurrency is a string of encrypted data representing a unit of currency monitored and organized by a peer-to-peer network known as a blockchain. In more simple terms, cryptocurrencies are a form of alternative payment created by using encryption algorithms. Because they use encryption technologies, they can work as currencies and virtual accounts.

You can use them for investment (in a loose sense) purposes as well as exchange products online. You can exchange real currency, such as the Pound Sterling, for "coins" and "tokens" of specific cryptocurrencies. It is estimated that there are over 12,000 cryptocurrencies at the time of writing this book. Between 2020 and 2022, the number of cryptocurrencies will grow at an incredible rate.

On the other hand, an NFT is a unique identifier that can cryptographically assign and prove ownership of digital goods. They are unique cryptographic tokens that exist on a blockchain, meaning they cannot be replicated. In simple terms, An NFT is a digital asset that represents real-world objects like art, music, in-game items, and videos. They are bought and sold online.

Cryptocurrencies and NFTs are not "real" businesses, and they have no backing, as the other investments discussed previously are. Values are intrinsic, meaning they are determined by how people think and not necessarily by the value themselves. At the same time, it may be argued that gold shares many of the same characteristics; you will agree that gold has come a long way, and it is virtually impossible for the general public to change their minds regarding its value.

Several online apps allow you to buy and sell both investments (again, used loosely). For NFTs, you can use AsyncArt, Axie Marketplace, Crypto.com, Decentraland, Foundation, KnownOrigin, LooksRare, and Magic Eden, while for cryptocurrencies, you can use Coinbase, Gemini, Binance, and eToro.

Consequently, the price fluctuates sporadically due to the above factors. For example, it has been reported at the time of writing this book that Logan Paul, a popular Youtuber, purchased a particular NFT in 2021 for $11,623,000, and it is now only worth $6. You read that correctly, eleven million six hundred twenty-three thousand dollars.

The current market for both currencies is unregulated. According to a recent report, the global crypto asset market value increased to USD 3 trillion at the end of 2021 but has declined to less than USD 1 trillion. As a result of this crash in value, consumers, investors, and financial systems are becoming increasingly concerned about the risks associated with digital assets. As a result of those risks, regulators are issuing statements to support regulatory oversight, aiming to achieve responsible innovation by understanding and balancing the downside risks and opportunities associated with digital assets. However, as long as this does not happen, the risk will likely remain, and these investments will remain unattractive.

This chapter has provided an overview of the various types of investments you can explore and invest in as you navigate your 9 to 5. There are, of course, other passive investments you can explore, including investments in startups. However, our discussion here has been limited to those investments that beginners can engage in.

CHAPTER THREE SUMMARY

Key points to keep in mind

- You can almost never go wrong with property investment.
- Gold investment is better as a store of value.
- Avoid buying single shares, ETF is a better idea.
- No matter the investment option you choose, do your research and investigation before you make any commitment.
- Investing is high risk, and you can lose your money.

CHAPTER FOUR
UNDERSTANDING INVESTMENT PATTERNS

We have discussed some of the characteristics and advantages associated with investing in previous chapters. The goal of this chapter is to continue exploring other fundamental patterns of investment, particularly the patterns of investing in stocks and shares. In order to provide you with a better understanding of these patterns, we will examine five of them.

This may seem obvious, but shares are traded in a stock market and stock exchanges. Before delving into the patterns, we will explain the difference between the stock exchange and the stock market, as these terms are used a lot in this chapter. The term stock market refers to a set of stocks that trade in a particular region or country. On the other hand, the term 'stock exchange' refers to the infrastructure or marketplace where equity trading occurs. We will use both words interchangeably.

Currently, there are about 60 major global stock exchanges that range in size and trading volume around the world. The ten most significant exchanges in the world, according to their size, are the New York Stock Exchange, NASDAQ, Tokyo Stock Exchange, Shanghai Stock Exchange, Hong Kong Stock Exchange, London Stock Exchange, Euronext, and Shenzhen Stock Exchange.

Using your apps for trading should not imply that trading occurs within the apps. Instead, the apps are connected to the various stock exchanges via their backends, and these exchanges complete the final transaction.

Investment Patterns

- **Market Rise and Fall**

    It is common for the value of shares to rise and fall. However, these movements are not usually catastrophic except during a market crash.

    A market crash occurs when the price of stocks drops suddenly and dramatically across a significant segment of a stock market, resulting in a substantial loss of wealth. Typically, these crashes are caused primarily by economic or political factors. However, in recent years, several crashes have occurred.

    Our most recent example occurred in 2022 due to the conflict between Russia and Ukraine. Prior to this, we also had one in 2008 as a result of an increase in global energy prices, which resulted in an increase in global inflation. The development resulted in many borrowers needing help repaying their mortgages. Therefore, property prices began to fall, resulting in a collapse in the value of financial institutions' assets. And there was another one in 2020 as a result of COVID-19.

- **Downturn Happens and Mostly Unpredictable**

    Knowing that stock markets undergo rises and fall, still, timing becomes unpredictable. If you are a beginner, it will be futile to attempt to predict when the next market crash will occur, although there are exceptions if you are an exceptional market analyst. It is not advisable to try to predict a market crash for most people, however.

In this section, we discuss the stock market's pattern, which helps you become more strategic in your investment trading.

As you are unable to predict the downturn, you may be wondering what steps you should take. The next point addresses this.

- **Market Recover and Generally Rise Over Time**

Regardless of how bad the crash is, the market will always recover. No matter how bad the impact is, the market will increase, more so if you have a diversified portfolio. We explained a diversified portfolio as having a proper mix of stock investments.

Different strategies are implemented by foreign countries to assist the market in recovering. Some countries have implemented a two-year strategy, while others, such as the UK market, had a five years plan to recover from the 2008 crash. When there are market crashes, government intervention is usually required since they are regulated. This is one advantage of shares over other forms of investments.

- **Long-term investing is the key**

    As a result of seeing these other patterns, it is relatively easy to understand why we advised that investing in stocks and shares should be done for the long term rather than as a temporary solution.

    It is almost always detrimental to your investment if you attempt to predict market movements by gambling with your shares in the short term.

As you read this, perhaps you are asking yourself how to proceed with maximizing your investment in the market and managing risks. That is what we are going to discuss in the next chapter.

CHAPTER FOUR SUMMARY

Key points to keep in mind

- Shares rise and fall.
- Recession or market downturn happens are they are mostly unpredictable.
- Market recover and generally rise over time.
- Always think long term when making shares investment.
- Investing is high risk, and you can lose your money.

CHAPTER FIVE
MANAGING INVESTMENT RISK

We will discuss in more detail some of the things we have mentioned previously so that you may understand what should be done in order to minimize the risk associated with investing in the stock market.

As there are several ways to manage the risks associated with investing in shares, I will explain risk briefly before delving into how to mitigate it and what the risks in the stock market are, as well as how to mitigate them.

Risk is a term widely used in the insurance industry to describe situations that involve exposure to danger. This is where you realize that some risks can be insured while others cannot. Examples of insurable risks include cars, houses and contents, life insurance, jewels, and so on. Examples of uninsurable risks include reputational, regulatory, trade secret, political, and pandemic risks. I have stated this at present because it is possible that in a few years, some, if not all, of these risks may be insurable.

As a result of the uncertainty and difficulty in predicting the outcome and impact of shares, investment is also classified as uninsurable. In most cases, individuals must bear the risks themselves since investing entails a certain degree of risk, which is why share investments cannot be insured.

Investing in shares involves the possibility of losing your money, which is valid for all types of investments. As a result, you may end up with less than what you put in, mainly if you only invest for the short term and do not appropriately diversify your portfolio.

Strategies For Managing Risks

- **Diversified Portfolio**

    As discussed throughout this book, the term "diversified" has been mentioned numerous times. What does it mean to have a diversified portfolio? It simply means having a variety of risks in one place. You may have shares in multiple industries in your budget, and the chances of all the industries experiencing an adverse event simultaneously are pretty slim, except in the case of a general economic recession. In addition to this, it is pretty much possible to have a portfolio (bucket) that includes stocks from different industries as well as shares from other geographic regions.

- **Dollar-Cost Averaging**

    The best way to make investing a habit is to invest regularly, such as monthly. This will ensure you always buy stocks regardless of the market. Experts refer to this as Dollar-Cost Averaging. By automating purchases, this investment strategy is able to simplify the process of dealing with uncertain markets. Regular investments are supported by dollar-cost averaging.

In the long run, you will not notice any rises or falls in your share value if you maintain this over time because your share value will continue to grow. Over time, diversified portfolio investment in an ETF returns at least 9% on average.

- **Invest for the Long haul**

In order for this to sink in, we have repeated it over and over again. Investing in shares is not a good idea if you intend to withdraw the money within the next ten years. Although some people recommend leaving your investment on for a period of five years, you will reap the most significant benefits when you leave it on for more than ten years. When you are able to accomplish this, you begin to truly appreciate the effort you have made.

Besides the apparent market crash that occurs repeatedly, you will benefit from compounding interest on your investment. I will explain how this works in more detail.

Upon purchase, you will likely receive a dividend payment and appreciate the value of your shares. All these funds earn returns when reinvested automatically, together with the monthly investments you make. Assuming the dividend/interest yielded 5% interest in the first year if reinvested; it is compounded to earn you higher interest, which is the beauty of the system.

- **Don't Panic**

Often, people need to pay attention to this point. When there is negative news about the market, they panic and sell their shares. There will always be speculation, and the market will usually respond accordingly. An example of this was when Elon Musk made a post on Twitter about a specific share, and the value of the share increased immediately.

This is because individuals can exert a significant influence on markets. There is no doubt that the comments made probably did not have any effect on the company itself, but due to people's emotional nature, they are quick to either buy or sell shares. However, over time and usually within a short period of time, the share price returns to where it was prior to the comments or even negative news.

It is essential to realize that any remarks made by a prominent individual will usually have an impact on the market that will prompt people to react; however, you need more grounds for you to respond. So hold your peace and let the market stabilize. It will always correct itself.

It is always advisable to allow time to ride out any market volatility. Market fluctuations are caused by panicked buying and selling. You will lose more money if you let spontaneity determine your share purchase strategy.

- **Don't disinvest when markets fall**

    This may seem obvious, but still worth mentioning. Do NOT take your money out when the market falls. It will rise again.

    The market autocorrects itself. The shares are a response to actual activities in which the companies are engaged. The results of these activities usually trigger any movements in the market. Because of this, you do not have to disinvest if you follow the news of the companies in which you hold shares, to ensure that they are doing well financially.

    You can cushion the adverse effects of subpar performance from one company to another by diversifying your portfolio. Therefore, we have emphasized diversifying your portfolio to compensate for any loss if one company performs poorly.

- **Consider Using a stop-loss order**
A stop-loss order is when you give an instruction to your app or stockbroker to sell your shares automatically when they reach a particular price.

Many investors give this order to reduce the risk of a sudden market downturn. It is also used to avoid selling unnecessarily during small fluctuations in the market. For example, setting a stop-loss order for 5% below the price at which you bought the stock will limit your loss to 5%, and it's generally advised to limit the order to 5% so that you don't sell prematurely and lose out on potential gains.

CHAPTER FIVE SUMMARY

Key points to keep in mind

- Consider dollar-cost averaging as a strategy.
- Don't forget to diversify your playlist
- Market recover and generally rise over time, don't panic, or disinvest when market falls.
- Always think long term when making shares investment.
- Investing is high risk, and you can lose your money.

CHAPTER SIX
FUNDS CATEGORISATION

There are various types of investment funds, which are broadly categorized into active, passive, and theme funds. This categorization facilitates the diversification of a portfolio. Portfolios are a grouping of funds to help manage risk.

Active investing involves active participation by a portfolio manager, fund manager, or other active participants. On the other hand, passive investing involves fewer transactions, such as purchasing index funds, exchange-traded funds, or other investment vehicles. By theme, this can include sectors, geographical locations, profit-focused, and environmental sustainability (ESG).

Themes
As per the Global Industry Classification Standard, there are eleven stock market sectors. We will

examine these categories and provide examples of shares within each category in the following paragraphs. Please note that this is not a recommendation for you to purchase any particular stock but rather some standards to assist you in making a decision.

- **Sector**

    Investments by sectors include healthcare, materials, real estate, consumer staples, consumer discretionary, utilities, energy, industrials, consumer services, financials, and technology. In a nutshell, when you buy shares by sector, you are spreading your risk as the chance of losing your funds because of issues in a particular industry is reduced.

    Below, we have given a further division and examples of companies in each sector.

- **Healthcare Sector**: These are companies that are pharmaceutical producers, manufacturers of medical devices, healthcare service providers, biotech, and Insurance companies. Examples are *Vertex Pharmaceuticals, Intuitive Surgical, UnitedHealth Group, and Teladoc Health.*

- **Materials Sector:** These involve construction materials, chemicals, paper, and glass, companies specializing in making paper and forest products, and Metals and mining companies. Examples of shares are *United States Steel Corp, Cleveland-Cliffs Inc., and Steel Dynamics Inc.*

- **Real estate Sector:** The companies here are involved in real estate and include real estate investment trusts (REITs), a particular category of public companies that own real estate. Examples are *Crown Castle International Corp. (CCI), Equinix, Inc.*

(EQIX), Public Storage (PSA), Prologis, Inc. (PLD), and American Tower Corporation (AMT).

- **Consumer Staples Sector:** These include companies involved in food, beverage, and tobacco, as well as producers of household goods and personal products. E.g., *Newell Brands Incorporated, Bunge Limited, and Newell Brands Incorporated.*

- **Discretionary Consumer Sector:** They include businesses in retail, eCommerce, hotel, luxury goods, and leisure and travel industries. Examples are *Nike, McDonald's, Disney, and Starbucks.*

- **Utility Sector**: These companies provide customers with utility services, such as water, electricity, and gas. Examples are *OGE Energy Corporation, NextEra Energy*

Incorporated, UGI Corporation, and NRG Energy Incorporated.

- **Energy Sector**: The companies in this category represent companies engaged in the exploration, production, refining, and sale of energy resources, including oil and natural gas, as well as companies that provide services to these industries. Examples are *Schlumberger Limited, Pioneer Natural Resources Company, and Marathon Petroleum Corporation.*

- **Industrials Sector:** These are companies involved in Industrial machinery construction and engineering, aerospace and defence, and electrical equipment. Examples are *Waste Management, Caterpillar, and 3M*

- **Communication services Sector:** They include wireless telecom network providers, media and entertainment companies, radio and television companies, and interactive media and internet companies. Examples are *Liberty Broadband Corporation, The Walt Disney Company,* and *Lumen Technologies Incorporated.*

- **Financials:** This includes investment banks, commercial banks, insurance companies, financial service providers, asset management companies, and financial brokers. Examples are *JPMorgan Chase, Berkshire Hathaway, and Lemonade.*

- **Technology Sector:** They include semiconductor producers, software and hardware providers, internet stocks, and cloud computing. Examples are *Apple Incorporated, Microsoft Corporation, and Meta Platforms Incorporated.*

- **Geography**

As a reminder, to get the best from your investment, it's essential to diversify, and diversification in geographical location is about spreading the risks. There are, therefore, opportunities to invest in countries that have an economy that is reasonably stable and steady, as well as opportunities to take a risk in investing in emerging markets. As a result, it is possible to compensate for the volatility of investing in a single economic region.

Examples of stocks in the regional or geographical locations are the FTSE 100 (UK), Baidu Incorporated (China), Alibaba Group Holding Limited (China), Vipshop holdings limited (China), Centrica Plc (UK), Engie SA (France), RWE AG (Germany), Nestle SA (Switzerland), Barrick Gold Corporation

(Canada), Mix Telematics Limited (South Africa) and Harmony Gold Mining Company (South Africa), or Jumia Technologies (Nigeria)

- **Income Focused**

These companies produce stable income and relatively reliable dividends for investors and are usually less volatile. Some of these companies pay dividends quarterly, bi-annually, or annually.

Examples of some of the best profit-focused shares are Microsoft, NextEra Energy, Verizon, and Waste Management.

- **ESG**

Environmental, Social, and Governance (ESG) refer to companies that comply with the principles of ESG. ESG is sometimes referred to as ethical investing because it is specifically targeted at investors who want to combine the profitability of their investments with ethical practices. A significant objective of ESG investing is to build a portfolio of companies demonstrating a commitment to corporate social responsibility and shareholder profit.

Additionally, some companies are addressing issues such as climate change, fair labour practices, and more transparent voluntary corporate governance disclosures. But, as you may have imagined, it is not an industry in and of itself. Instead, it consists of companies in other industries that adhere to the tenets of the environmental, social, and governance movement.

- **Active Investing**

    This is the second categorization of investment and involves the continuous buying and selling of shares by the investor or on their behalf by a fund manager. We have outlined some of the characteristics below.

- **Investors or their fund managers are constantly making decisions.**

    Because they are always buying or selling, they constantly decide to either buy or sell to take advantage of the opportunity. As a result, each investment in a fund manager's portfolio is evaluated by a wide range of data. This includes quantitative and qualitative information about the stocks as well as information about broader economic and market trends.

- **Research and Intuition**

    The market is dynamic, and staying ahead of the curve requires constant research. Therefore, they conduct extensive research and sometimes intuition. Their decisions need to be infallible since billions of dollars can be lost or acquired within seconds. Therefore, research is required. Primarily, their intuition results from their experience, which is why they are better positioned to make educated guesses, and sometimes those guesses have been successful.

- **Higher charges**

    As a result of the time and experience involved, the participant in active investing charge more for their services; however, whether they are worth it is a question you can ask, as some have generated negative returns in the last couple of years because of the impact of COVID-19 and the Russian-Ukraine war. Thus, we recommend that you conduct due diligence before outsourcing your funds to a fund manager or passive investments.

- **Passive Investing**

Unlike active investing, passive is an investment that doesn't review much research; it's also an investment that can be done relatively by anyone and cost a lot less.

Other characteristics are that they need to be managed more closely and can quickly be done through an investment app. Although we have said that extensive research is not necessary here, it's still essential to examine the performance trend of the stocks you are looking to buy before buying.

When moving away from passive investments, ensure you fully understand how the market works and have good reasons to do so.

CHAPTER SIX SUMMARY

Key points to keep in mind

- Select from the sector that best suits you and that you understand.

- Investing in other geography can be a way to diversify your portfolio.

- You may want to consider using a fund manager because of the advantages.

- Don't let emotions guide your choice of shares to buy.

- Investing is high risk, and you can lose your money.

CHAPTER SEVEN
COMMON PITFALL IN INVESTING

Having now understood what investing is and how to invest, it is crucial for you to understand what mistakes to avoid when investing. Furthermore, to ensure you avoid repeating the same mistakes over and over again, it is essential that you keep these points in mind and review them periodically.

As the old saying goes, it's unwise to continue doing the same thing and expect a different outcome. Therefore, if you make any of these mistakes, consider reexamining your strategy and taking appropriate action.

- **Using someone else's expectations or approach.**

    This is a mistake that new entrants to the investment world make. Just because someone you know is trading on a stock doesn't mean you should do the same.

There are several things that could go wrong. For example, they may have yet to inform you of everything they are doing; they may also have a different risk appetite than you. They may be investing for a more extended period of time than you. You may be interested in shares that will yield more value over time if they have a different expectation, such as income-focused. Ensure that you understand your expectations and take an approach that will satisfy those expectations.

- **Not Diversified Enough or Diversifying Too Much**

The word "diversify" has been repeatedly used in the book, which was intended to emphasize the importance of having a well-rounded and balanced portfolio. This word has been explained almost everywhere it is mentioned.

As you are aware, we discussed in chapter six the different investing categories and highlighted them according to geographical location, sector, etc. The best companies in any industry and geography will almost guarantee a diversified portfolio if you purchase shares in these companies or an ETF that combines different sectors.

Even though diversification has its advantages, there is also a risk of excessive diversification, which occurs if you buy the FTSE 100 and then invest in one of its constituent companies separately.

- **Trying to Time the Market**

    In spite of the fact that we live in an age of free information, there are still many items of information that need to be purchased by the individual investor, and some information you cannot access as an individual investor. It may become difficult to determine when to buy and sell because of this.

    Dollar-cost averaging is the solution, as discussed earlier (see page 73). The key is to invest consistently, no matter how small the amount.

- **Buying Shares in a Business You Don't Understand**

    As part of our discussion on ESG, we discussed the choice of some investors to invest only in ethical firms. Investing should be deliberate. Do not invest in companies you do not know about or don't fully understand. Even if you hear that they are making profits, those profits may be a bubble. As they say, all that glitters is not always gold.

It is essential to take the time to learn a few things about the companies that you are considering before making any financial commitments.

- **Impatience**

    As investing is a long-term endeavor, beginners are advised to invest in index funds or exchange-traded funds. However, it is essential to be patient when investing in these classes of shares since they usually do not yield returns in the first few years, especially during recessions or other events that can lead to market imbalances.

Between 2000 and 2021, the S&P 500 index returned an average of 9% annually. So please don't panic; it will eventually pay off.

- **Using Monies that You Cannot Afford to Lose**

Investing in shares is one of those risks that cannot be insured against, which is why it is essential to invest only what you can afford to lose. As loose as this statement may seem, it is the truth.

It is essential to know your risk appetite and what you are willing to accept. How much money can you lose and still be okay with?

Investing is not a competition, so you should focus on what is important to you. Be aware of what others are doing but be cautious of being influenced by their BIG moves.

- **Emotional Investing**

    It is not appropriate to invest based on emotions. Develop a plan, not rely on hunches; you are not an expert. If you feel an undue attachment to a particular company, ask yourself why. Do not act on emotion. The truth is that emotions are temporary feelings, and it is possible that you have already lost your investment before you realize it. Maintain a business-like attitude.

- **Too High Expectations**

    It is essential to understand that investing is neither gambling nor a get-rich-quick scheme. If you are investing, please keep in mind that your capital may be at risk and that you are in it for the long haul.

It is similar to eating a meal, which does not manifest its effect immediately. However, with time, it becomes increasingly apparent that the impact of eating has occurred. The same applies to shares. It may take some time before it begins delivering expected returns, sometimes longer than expected and sometimes less than what you expect. There is no guarantee.

The goal should be to conduct adequate research and prepare a strategy in order to minimize loss or to live with the decisions you have made. And always remember that the higher the risk in an investment, the higher the level of returns that is expected from it.

- **Not Talking with Experts**

    As the saying goes, no man is an island. An expert doesn't necessarily have to be someone you need to pay for their services, but someone you know who knows a few things about investing.

    Be bold and ask questions. Consult widely. You might miss something that a second set of eyes would be able to see.

    As crucial as being independent is when you make this decision, make sure you do not isolate yourself during the process.

- **Not Investing or starting late**

    If, after reading all the chapters of this book and you move on with life as if nothing happened, you would have done more injustice to the time invested for both of us.

You didn't come this far not to act; the best action you can take now is to start. Don't wait until everything is all well and good. As you already know, there will always be new challenges and things that will compete for your resources.

The power of compound interest is enhanced when you begin early, as we discussed earlier (See page 15). The earlier you start, the more excellent your opportunity to maximize the benefits of compounding interest.

If you act now and start early, your future self will thank you. Here's your chance.

CHAPTER SEVEN SUMMARY

Key points to keep in mind

- If you do not invest at all or invest later, you will lose out on the power of compound interest.
- Maintaining a diversified investment portfolio is the most important concept to understand as a beginner.
- Avoid investing in stocks you do not understand.
- Set a reasonable expectation and don't base your expectations on other people result
- Don't risk more than you can afford to lose.
- Investing is high risk, and you can lose your money.

ABOUT THE BOOK

Investing is a vehicle through which you can overcome the limitations of time. It is not the time itself that is limited but the amount of time people have at their disposal. We must invest for this reason.

No matter how much a person earns, they can only meet their needs if paid by the hour. In economics, it is said that human needs are limitless, but the means of meeting those needs are not. Consequently, some people work additional shifts or hours to meet those needs. However, due to their limited time available, it's advisable that they devise a method to ensure that their money is secure and productive while they are not working.

There are a number of practical and actionable recommendations in the book that can assist you in starting to invest immediately.

ABOUT THE AUTHOR

Ephraim Unuigbe is a chartered accountant and a career and personal finance coach. The author holds a BSc in Accounting, as well as membership in the Institute of Chartered Accountants of Nigeria and certification as a Certified Information Systems Auditor by the Information Systems Audit and Control Association, among other credentials.

Ephraim is currently employed with one of the top accounting firms in the United Kingdom, where he provides assurance services to corporate entities. Also, Ephraim serves as Director of Corporate Governance on the board of HACTRI (a Nigerian literacy organization). Also, he is a board member of the Itchen Sixth Form College in the United Kingdom.

Ephraim is married to Marian Unuigbe and has two children, Daniel Chukwudi and Eseohen Elizabeth.

ACKNOWLEDGEMENT

To my most important companion, counselor, helper, intercessor, advocate, strengthener, and standby, the Holy Spirit. Thank you.

OTHER BOOKS BY THE AUTHOR TO DATE

- Succeeding in your career - A Roadmap for Graduates & Young Professionals

- Let's talk about money - A guide to Personal Finances for Young Adults

- How to choose a career path - A Spiritual Perspective to Career Choice & Life

- Managing Family Finance - for Career Couples

- Career & Romance - How to Find Your Soul Mate as a Single Career Professional

- The Career Woman's Guide to SINGLE PARENTING: For Single Female Career Professionals with teenage kids between the ages of 12 -19.

All are available on amazon.com and ephraim-unuigbe.online

Contact the author via info@ephraim-unuigbe.online or ephraim.unuigbe@gmail.com

SERVICES WE OFFER

Career Counselling
We assist individuals of all ages in clarifying and attaining their career goals. We also teach students the development of learner-centered skills they can utilize in their academic careers and life beyond.

Personal Finance Coaching
Personal finance refers to how well people adhere to a budget when managing their finances. Over time, the goal is to save money while also spending money on needed resources and allocating a particular amount for each living expense. With my guidance, you will learn how to make, manage, and multiply your money.

CV Review and Writing
The modern world of employment demands that your CV stands out, and we provide a range of services through which our professional CV writers can create the CV just for you. Every CV we create is tailored specifically to meet your needs.

Cover Letter and Personal Statement
We will provide you with a professional who knows how to write you a high-performing letter for your job application or personal statement. Paired with our professionally written CV, you can differentiate yourself from other applicants.

LinkedIn Profile Optimization

You can take your LinkedIn profile to the next level and turn it into a powerful career tool that highlights your abilities and experiences and impresses your contacts.

Interview Coaching

Our professionals help you be the best candidate your potential employer has ever seen. A well-rounded approach that addresses the verbal and non-verbal factors.

www.ingramcontent.com/pod-product-compliance
Lightning Source LLC
Chambersburg PA
CBHW070242220526
45465CB00004B/1484